ABANDONED SAN ANTONIO

RUINS OF THE ALAMO CITY

JOE RIZZO

AMERICA
THROUGH TIME®
ADDING COLOR TO AMERICAN HISTORY

America Through Time is an imprint of Fonthill Media LLC
www.through-time.com
office@through-time.com

Published by Arcadia Publishing by arrangement with Fonthill Media LLC
For all general information, please contact Arcadia Publishing:
Telephone: 843-853-2070
Fax: 843-853-0044
E-mail: sales@arcadiapublishing.com
For customer service and orders:
Toll-Free 1-888-313-2665

www.arcadiapublishing.com

First published 2022

ISBN 978-1-63499-387-6

Typeset in Trade Gothic 10pt on 15pt
Printed and bound in England

CONTENTS

ABOUT THE AUTHOR

Exploring abandoned buildings has been a hobby for Joe Rizzo for over twenty years. Joe grew up in Tucson, Arizona, and has been living in San Antonio since 1998. About ten years ago, Joe came up with the idea to produce a book about abandoned structures after coming across the book *The New American Ghetto* written by Camilo Jose Vergara. This book inspired Joe to document the many vacant buildings around San Antonio before they were renovated or demolished in the name of progress.

INTRODUCTION

Finding and exploring abandoned buildings has been a fascination for me since I was a teenager. This hobby, though perilous and illegal, has provided me with many worthwhile experiences. The first abandoned building I explored, over twenty-five years ago, was in Tucson, Arizona. It was the former "colored school" during the days of segregation. After segregation ended in 1951, the school served as a junior high until 1978, when it was ordered to be closed. When I walked around inside the building, I found hundreds of textbooks in the hallways and classrooms. I found out later that the school was being used by the local school district as a warehouse for textbooks.

After moving to San Antonio in 1998, I noticed many abandoned buildings around the city. My desire to explore them was not a priority at the time. Around ten years ago, while at the library, I found a book titled *The New American Ghetto* by Camilo Jose Vergara. This photo-essay book showed the evolution of the rundown areas of U.S. cities such as Detroit, Chicago, Gary, and Brooklyn. After perusing the book, I found my fascination with abandoned buildings reignited. Shortly thereafter, I purchased a pocket-sized digital camera and started documenting the derelict structures around San Antonio. In the years since, I upgraded to a Canon DSLR and have spent a lot of time exploring the interiors of abandoned buildings, including factories, schools, and houses. Thanks to the Internet and social media, I have been able to network with like-minded people. I have been caught trespassing several times, but usually I am just given a warning by the police or security guards assigned to patrol vacant structures. My hobby as an urban explorer has given me the opportunity to see what most people will never experience.

1

FEDERAL JAIL

O riginally built as the Bexar County Jail in 1962, this building housed federal inmates from 1987-2019. Inspections by local government officials were done in recent years and the building was declared to have unsatisfactory conditions. The former correctional center was ordered by a county judge to be demolished. In late 2020, demolition began on the downtown jail, and it was completely razed by April 2021.

In all my years of exploring abandoned buildings, I never thought I would have the opportunity to see the inside of an abandoned jail. Walking around this building gave me the chills when thinking of the thousands of inmates that were housed here over the last six decades. It was amazing to see the old-fashioned metal bars and relics of prison life.

Above: An old-school boom box was left behind on the counter inside this jail.

Left: The walk-in cooler looks inviting, but I declined the offer.

Eerie reminders of prison life.

The inside of a jail pod on one of the upper floors.

"Think safety" reminded me to be aware of my surroundings inside this massive building.

The metal door sits wide open in this area of the jail.

Walk-in coolers helped store food for staff and inmates alike.

Kitchen equipment sits deep in the caverns of the facility.

Conditions inside the jail were unbearable in the twilight years of this structure.

Bunk bed metal frames line the interior of this cell.

Massive laundry machines were left behind.

The lifespan of this jail was relatively short compared to other detention facilities around the country.

Demolition work is evident on an upper floor of the jailhouse.

2

PRO PLUS MILLS

Opened in 1916 by the Guenther family under the name Liberty Mills, this massive grain factory is littered with debris and the pockmarked windows have suffered decades of vandalism. The most recent tenant of the property was P & M Products. This old grain mill sits along railroad tracks and is frequented by homeless people that roam the area. It is currently owned by a bail bonds company which operates next door to this former factory. Efforts by the bail bondsman to demolish the grain mill have been halted by local preservationists. There have been rumors of people being killed inside the structure. Evidence of drug use by homeless people is scattered around the premises.

Sitting just west of downtown, the decaying grain mill towers over the adjacent railroad tracks.

The last tenant of the property, P & M Products, used the building to manufacture yeast and grain products.

Graffiti decorates this wall inside the property.

Various items have been sitting unused for years in this room of the mill.

A mound of dirt and broken pieces of concrete sit inside a former storage building.

Above: The stacks that were once utilized to produce grain and other feed products show decades of neglect and decay.

Right: This building on the property may have been used for storage of grain.

3

HOT WELLS HOTEL

Well-known in the late nineteenth century for its hot sulfur springs, this former luxury resort sits as a crumbling shell of its former self. In the early 1900s, many movie stars, athletes, and dignitaries visited or stayed at this hotel. During this period, the resort was still in an undeveloped area and was reached from downtown San Antonio by streetcar. The property once housed a movie studio that produced several films. Three major fires struck the building, the first occurring in 1925. A second blaze in 1988 was caused by a lightning strike and devastated the structure. The third major fire happened in 1997.

A major fire in 1997 left this once luxurious hotel in ruins.

The natatorium was divided into three sections, one for men, one for women, and the middle pool for families.

The hotel property is owned by local entrepreneur James Lifshutz and has recently been redeveloped as a public park.

In the summer of 2014, I was given a tour around the interior of the ruins by Justin Parr, the caretaker.

4

ST. JOHN'S SEMINARY

This former school was used to educate Catholic high school students from 1915 to 1972. The campus of St. John's Seminary was converted to a drug treatment facility shortly thereafter. The property, which consisted of eight buildings, was used by the Patrician Movement until 2011. After the Patrician Movement vacated the premises, the buildings were left open to the elements and vandalism. Renovation of some of the buildings into apartments started in 2018. Two of the buildings—the chapel and the cafeteria—remain abandoned.

I have explored this property several times and found many interesting relics dating back to the time when the school was operated for Catholic children, including desks, bedframes, and trophies. One time while exploring the school with some friends, we were spotted by a security guard in the courtyard area. We managed to exit the property quickly without being arrested. After this harrowing encounter, my friends decided never to explore this place again. I have returned a few times to this place and documented the progress of the repurposing of the former school buildings.

An old classroom building on the property sat empty for many years before renovation.

A chalkboard inside a classroom defaced with graffiti.

A piano sits on the stage inside the auditorium.

Fire evidence inside one of the buildings.

The stained-glass windows inside the chapel of the seminary school. Surprisingly, the windows never displayed signs of vandalism even though other buildings on the school property were damaged heavily by vandals.

Inside the auditorium are curtains and other stage items left behind.

The swimming pool was filled with stagnant water when I took this photo in 2017. After renovation of the property commenced, this pool was filled in and paved over, leaving no trace behind of the pool or the changing rooms.

5

TURTLE CREEK EVENT CENTER

Originally the main building for a golf course when it was opened in 1970, this building was renovated in the late 1980s into a ballroom. Part of the building operated as a nightclub during the 1990s and 2000s. After several violent incidents, including a deadly shooting, the nightclub was ordered by the city to close in 2009. The structure suffered a major fire in November 2016 and was demolished in early 2017. I explored this massive building twice before the devastating fire. The fire was believed to have been started by people squatting inside the building who were trying to stay warm during a bitterly cold winter. After the fire, I returned a few times to check out the building. I remember going to this nightclub when it was open for business back in the late 1990s/early 2000s.

This area of the nightclub had its exterior walls torn down not long after it went out of business.

Right: Looking down from the third floor on the flights of stairs littered with debris.

Below: The entrance to the nightclub was lined with stone archways.

An eerie view of the ruins shortly before the nightclub was demolished. The fire that racked the former event center left the roof falling in and ashes everywhere.

Looking down from the balcony at the devastation of the fire.

6

CAR DEALERSHIP

This former car dealership has lots of graffiti and extensive vandalism. It is likely that the recession of 2008-09 led to the closure of this building. I have explored this place at least twenty times due to the ease of entrance. One time I found a mattress in one of the rooms along with a blanket and dirty clothing. During one of my visits to this abandoned facility I found surveillance cameras in the parking lot and learned that the building was armed with a security alarm. This was in 2019, so it surprised me that it took the owners so long to finally secure the property against trespassers and vandals. I returned to explore the dealership in July 2021 and found that the surveillance equipment had been removed from the property. The main building suffered a major fire recently, and there were several homeless people hanging out inside the structure.

Looking downstairs from the second floor of this former dealership. Lots of debris and graffiti have accumulated over the ten years that this building has been abandoned.

Fire evidence on the exterior of the structure. I first explored this dealership in 2016 and have seen it get progressively worse over the years.

The ceiling panels are falling in in this area of the building.

Graffiti lines the drywall in this hallway.

Ashes litter this part of the service facility in the dealership.

A wheelbarrow lies discarded on the property.

The garage doors sit halfway open with graffiti displayed on the exterior walls. The juxtaposition of a derelict structure in the foreground with a modern glass tower in the background contrasts quite nicely.

When I explored this dealership in July 2021, I encountered several homeless people inside the buildings. They mentioned that the structures may be demolished soon. The condition of the property makes it unsalvageable and tearing down the buildings will cost less money compared to renovating it.

7

FRIEDRICH REFRIGERATION PLANT

Friedrich Refrigeration was founded in 1883 by Ed Friedrich. Friedrich was an innovator whose legacy left a major impact on San Antonio. As a craftsman, Friedrich liked to produce furniture from the horns of longhorn cattle. By the 1950s, the company was a leading producer of commercial refrigeration equipment. The plant produced 500 floating air window units in 1952. The first large-scale plant for this company was opened on East Commerce Street in 1923. This factory was built in stages over the years.

The east side plant was closed in 1990 and operations were moved to a new facility on the northeast side. This massive plant has slowly deteriorated since the shutting down of operations. There was an effort to revitalize the property in the early 2000s. Several businesses were opened on the first floor of the building, but the companies had to vacate the premises after the building was condemned by health officials.

The refrigeration plant property was inspected for chemical residue when developers announced plans to revitalize the former factory in 2001.

The massive structure has many hidden rooms.

The wooden roof has collapsed in this area of the plant after years of natural decay.

In this room, the wooden floor remains intact.

Graffiti artists have left their mark in the vacant factory's numerous rooms.

A sign left behind reads, "Merchandising at its best," and leans right side up inside an office.

Wide-open spaces were necessary for the manufacturing and storage of refrigeration units and air-conditioner machines.

Industrial hoses hang from the wall in this area of the plant.

A table with dining items sits in a flooded room.

Rusted paint cans and other items crowd around this tool room.

This sign hangs off the wall in what is believed to be the welding room.

The conveyor belt once used for transporting units around the factory.

Freight elevator shaft that has been sitting long unused inside the plant.

This staircase is in relatively good condition after three decades of neglect.

8

ROEGELEIN PROVISION CO.

The company's first meat processing plant was located next door to its first meat market on Commerce Street. This plant, built in 1932, was designed with a capacity of 3,000 pounds. As time went on and business picked up, the owner, Wilhelm Roegelein, opened a second plant just west of downtown. Roegelein chose the site because of its proximity to the Union Stock Yards. The property occupied four acres and was adjacent to two railroad tracks. The meat plant was designed with ultra-modern features, including stainless steel walls. A third plant was opened at 1900 South Laredo Street, just around the corner from the Brazos Street location. The company sold its operations to another firm in the 1980s. Stiff competition from other major meatpacking companies caused Roegelein to shut down in 1990 and the buildings sat vacant for many years. One of the buildings suffered a major fire in 2009 and was demolished shortly thereafter. An ice company currently operates out of one of the buildings on the premises.

Graffiti decorates the outer wall of this warehouse on the property.

This facility was one of the biggest producers of meat products in the country for decades.

Above: Generations of local residents worked for this company. My grandfather and other relatives worked here for many years.

Left: An old warehouse with an old metal staircase and broken windows sits forsaken on the property.

9

RACETRACK

L ocated on the outskirts of San Antonio, this racetrack's final season was in 2007. The half-mile raceway opened for business in 1977 and drew large crowds for major racing events for about thirty years. After the official closing, there was a brief resurrection in 2012 when about 120 racers participated in Octoberfast. It was estimated that almost 5,000 race car fans attended the event. The racetrack's director of operations announced in late 2012 that races would resume for the 2013 racing season. News articles do not indicate that stock car races were held in 2013 or any subsequent seasons. The racetrack has been sitting forlorn since 2012 and it is unknown if there are any future plans for the property.

The stands that seated crowds for decades and the announcer's box sit forlorn in a rural area just outside of San Antonio.

The concrete racetrack has sat unused for almost ten years.

Weeds grow along the pavement that was once used for stock-car races.

The wooden bleachers slowly deteriorate in the brutal climate of south Texas.

Left: This stand slowly collects rust and may have been where the flagman sat.

Below: A tree grows in the middle of the bleachers where racing fans once observed the events.

Right: The racetrack is watched by an excavating company that operates next door. Once when I was exploring this place I was approached by a not-so-friendly man in a truck who may have been the owner of the property.

Below: Here sits the ticket booth that has been unused for many years.

10

ICE FACTORY

This long-vacant factory was full of mold from the years of ice production. The ice and cold-storage company was founded in 1909. Ice production was vital for the South Texas region due to the humid climate. Storage of furs and seal skins in refrigerated spaces also were important for local residents. The company's production grew rapidly in its early years. As production grew, the factory added floor space and erected new buildings. It is unknown when the company ceased production. Some of the buildings were later used by a meat-packing firm. Renovation of the property started in 2019. One of the vacant warehouses on the premises was used for several years as a music venue.

This ladder leading upstairs appears very unsteady.

Wearing a face mask was necessary because the air quality inside this factory was dismal.

These electrical boxes have suffered decades of natural decay and rust.

A wide-open hallway leads to a dark chamber in this massive plant.

Piles of debris inside another room in the former ice factory.

Evidence of mold and natural decay can be seen in this room.

The first accessible room upon entering the vacant factory had large cement blocks that were possibly used for ice storage. I found a sleeping bag in this area of the room, but fortunately I did not encounter any squatters.

11

WAREHOUSES/INDUSTRIAL

There are many abandoned warehouses and industrial facilities around San Antonio. Some of these buildings are easy to enter and have a lot of material left behind. Just west of downtown there is a row of massive warehouses along two city blocks. I have tried gaining access to these warehouses, but they are secured tightly. I have encountered homeless people a few times when exploring warehouses. They usually don't bother me as long as I let them know that I'm not a security guard.

This incinerator sits unused outside a warehouse on the north side of San Antonio.

Furniture and various items litter this room inside the warehouse facility.

This construction site has been sitting unfinished since early 2020.

Signs on the property indicate that a car dealership was to be operated in this building.

Steel beams and metal pipes were left behind by the project managers.

This downtown building suffered a major fire in early 2020. The burnt structure was demolished shortly thereafter.

Right: I encountered homeless people while exploring the interior of this building.

Below: This former pallet warehouse was transformed into an outdoor art gallery in 2017.

Colorful murals by local artists decorate the exterior walls of these buildings.

This warehouse was used for many decades for storage.

Though the property is used for art festivals, some of the buildings sit unused, including this structure.

This building's upper exterior resembles the façade of the Alamo.

Inside one of the warehouses sits a pile of debris along with industrial items.

The pallet company vacated the premises in 2016 and left many items behind inside the warehouses.

Graffiti decorates the exterior of this building on the former pallet warehouse property.

This meat-packing warehouse closed down in 2014.

Left: The security gate on the property of the former meat plant is slowly being reclaimed by nature.

Below: A combination of factors led to the shuttering of this meat factory, including an ongoing drought, competition, and a dwindling supply of cattle.

Right: It was not fun walking around inside this sweltering warehouse. Many industrial items made of metal and the corrugated metal walls magnified the heat inside the building.

Below: A stripped and rusty car sits inside a storage area.

Left: Hundreds of items were left behind inside this warehouse on the south side.

Below: This wooden spiral staircase lies discarded on its side.

Shortly after I explored this warehouse, the building was demolished in the summer of 2021.

Huge fans line the upper part of this former dry-cleaning facility. It is unknown from doing research when this company shuttered its operations. The dry-cleaning opened for business in 1945.

Laundry machines sit in the corner of this mammoth area.

Long gone are the glass windows of the dry-cleaning company offices.

Natural light illuminates the interior thanks to the huge windows on the upper level of the building. I was only able to explore this building once in early 2017. The laundry facility was secured tightly shortly thereafter and outfitted with security cameras.

This shell of a warehouse building is located on San Antonio's south side. A major fire occurred on this property in 2014.

Above: Fire stains are evident on this limestone wall. This building housed the first Texaco gas station in San Antonio and was most recently used by a local digital marketing firm. A major fire gutted this structure and the neighboring business in February 2020.

Left: Graffiti marks the interior of the structure.

The ruins of the building have been left standing since the fire and it is unknown if there are plans to tear down the façade or rebuild it in the future.

This historic building sitting in ruins is passed daily by thousands of vehicles since it sits at a major intersection on San Antonio's south side.

Bricks and debris litter the interior of this former tortilla factory.

I explored the inside of this abandoned tortilla factory in 2015. It was not easy to get inside, because most of the building was locked up tight. The building was completely demolished in late 2020.

Weeds and other plants grow through the concrete of this former car repair shop.

This mural sits faded on the interior wall of the vacant garage.

A possible art structure topped by a mailbox on the property of the repair shop.

Overlooking the courtyard of the property is possibly the storage building or the office of the repair garage.

Exterior wall of the garage still topped with signs advertising the services once provided by the business.

12

RESIDENTIAL

Abandoned residential properties can be found all over San Antonio, whether in upscale neighborhoods or in areas that are riddled with poverty and crime. These properties are prime locations for drug usage and squatters. I am fortunate that I have never encountered these types of situations while exploring abandoned houses. One time I was caught trespassing by the police while exploring an abandoned mansion. The officers gave me a warning and let me go after I showed them my camera and explained that I take photos of derelict properties as a hobby. One of the officers even suggested that I check out an abandoned grain mill near downtown.

Located in a rural area just outside of San Antonio, this house looks like the residents left one day and never came back for their belongings.

Dishes and other personal items remain on the kitchen counter.

This forsaken chair sits on the second floor of a vacant house and hearkens back to the forgotten memories that haunt the structure.

Nature is slowly taking over this kitchen.

The collapse of civilization ran through my mind while exploring this forlorn place. Trailer parks are symbolized as the bottom rung of society, the place where nobody wants to be.

These abandoned trailers were patrolled by stray dogs and surrounded by discarded mattresses.

Above: An old Toyota stripped down and sitting on blocks outside a trailer.

Left: An almost empty bedroom, save discarded personal items.

Above: These abandoned apartments are overgrown with weeds and sit wide open to the elements. The complex has been vacant since 2018.

Right: An old-school tube television amongst piles of debris inside this abandoned mansion. I was caught by the police while taking photos on the second floor of this house. They gave me a warning after seeing that I wasn't burglarizing the place or causing vandalism.

Hidden deep in the woods sits this collection of houses that have been abandoned since the 1970s. It is unknown why these houses were vacated. Research of this property yielded little information.

Trekking through the forest to find these houses was not easy. There were mosquitoes flying around and spider webs were spread between adjacent trees.

It surprised me that even though these houses are hidden in the woods, there were no wild animals roaming in the structures.

Limestone was used in the construction of some of these houses. This architecture method has helped the structures remain intact for decades.

Natural decay is evident in this forlorn residence.

Some of the houses were covered with spider webs which discouraged me from entering the units. Here we see an old couch left behind for years.

A huge pile of furniture sits inside this wide-open house. It appears to be a dumping ground for unwanted items.

Hopefully these houses can be restored in the future and put to good use instead of being left to rot or eventually torn down.

13

TEXTILE MILL

L ocated in a small town just north of San Antonio, this massive factory was used to film several episodes of *Fear the Walking Dead*. The building housing the former textile mill takes up over 500,000 square feet. It served as one of the largest employers in this community for several generations. The plant first started operations in 1921. After a few years, the company declared bankruptcy and was reorganized in 1931. Textiles produced by the factory in the early 1940s were utilized for the war effort. The company expanded into retail business after World War II. Layoffs caused by dependence on lower-priced textile imports started in the 1990s with the eventual shuttering of the plant. The textile mill shut down in 2005 and has been awaiting redevelopment since then.

Above: An exterior wall displays graffiti by local taggers.

Right: This shelf holds various items inside a storage building.

Peeling paint and debris can be seen inside this massive room.

A rusty fire hydrant surrounded by plants.

Wide-open rooms provided sufficient space for storage of textiles and production machines.

Broken windows pockmark this building on the property.

Chairs, tables, and desks left behind. It is unbelievable how many discarded items I have found in vacant buildings that can be put to better use.

A rusty machine left outside a building on the premises.

An old-fashioned textile machine left behind inside one of the buildings.

A pallet on top of a shelf collecting dust.

This building sits along the river and housed the water pump that provided electricity for the textile factory.

CLOSING THOUGHTS

Finding abandoned places to explore has never been a problem for me. There are many more vacant properties in San Antonio which are not covered in this book such as the Longhorn Quarry, Lone Star Brewery, and a hospital that served the black community during the days of segregation.

One place I will always regret not exploring is the Protestant Children's Home. This former orphanage was built in 1926 in northwest San Antonio. I lived not far from this vacant property for several years and would walk by it occasionally when going to the nearby post office. Sometimes I would peek in the windows and see interesting remnants, but I never had time to go inside and explore the building. When I finally brought a camera in 2012, I decided to try exploring the former children's home, but it was demolished before I had a chance. The land on which the orphanage occupied was redeveloped into a shopping center, which includes a Walmart.

It is a shame that a historic relic of San Antonio was erased in the name of progress. The San Antonio Conservation Society is a local organization that has fought hard to preserve many historic buildings in San Antonio from being demolished. I am grateful for the efforts of this organization in making sure that historic places are not forgotten or torn down.

BIBLIOGRAPHY

Cobb, Chris. "New Life for Old Mill." *New Braunfels Herald-Zeitung*, 9 January 2008.

Danini, Carmina. "Roegelein devoted himself to family business - His grandparents started the slaughtering company in 1905." *San Antonio Express-News*, 28 January 2004, p. 6B.

Gonzalez, John W. "Bexar plans retirement for old jail." *San Antonio Express-News*, 7 October 2015, expressnews.com/news/local/article/Bexar-plans-retirement-for-old-jail-6554623.php.

Huddleston, Scott. "Panel moves to save old flour mill; 1916 structure is a landmark near downtown." *San Antonio Express-News*, 16 January 2014, p. 4A.

Hunt, Paula. "San Antonio's orphanages evolved in outlook, organization." *San Antonio Express-News*, 24 August 2008, p. 4H.

Laurel, Lety and Edmundo Conchas. "Hope for Rebirth." *San Antonio Express-News*, 14 December 2005, p. 1SE.

Mabrito, Bruce. "S.A.-area motor sports; Car racetracks roared, later faded; Since 1900, many tracks hosted various race categories; last facility folded after four events in 2012-13." *San Antonio Express-News*, 7 July 2015, p. 4A.

Morton, Neal. "Friedrich's new site is pretty cool." *San Antonio Express-News*, 10 April 2014, p. 1B.

Pesquera, Adolfo. "Global Crossing is set to bring network to S.A." *San Antonio Express-News*, 2 March 2001, p. 2E.

"St. John's Begins Last Activities." *San Antonio Express*, 6 May 1972, p. 5-B.